GARRY BUSHELL is the top
TV critic, read by nearly eleven million
people five days a week in The Sun. Son
of a fireman, Garry was born and raised in South
East London, and started his journalistic career on
the rock weekly Sounds in 1978. He wrote the
best-selling biography of Iron Maiden, called
Running Free, and a series of successful
magazines, including Dance Craze: The 2-Tone
Story, before making his Fleet Street debut in
1985. Garry worked at the Daily Mirror and the
London Evening Standard before landing a staff
job on The Sun, editing the pop and showbiz
column 'Bizarre'. Here he conceived and
organised the Number One single, "Let It Be" by
Ferry Aid, in 1987, which raised over £1 million
for the families of the Zeebrugge ferry disaster
victims - with the help of Paul McCartney,
Michael Jackson, Mark Knopfler and scores of top
pop stars. Garry has been TV Editor and Show-
business Editor of The Sun, and Assistant Editor
of The Daily Star. But he is best known for his
hard-hitting TV column, Bushell On The Box.
Garry starred in the cult hit Sky TV variety show,
Saturday Night, and has appeared on scores of TV
shows including Telly Addicts, Star Test, Whistle
Test, Noel's House Party, Kilroy, 16-Up, and
Central Weekend Live. Garry is married with three
children.

1

© Kingsfleet Publications 1992

Cartoons by Max

ISBN 1 874130 17 5

Printed and bound in Great Britain

Published by Kingsfleet Publications
The Power House, Tandridge Court Farm,
Tandridge Lane, Oxted, Surrey RH8 9NJ

Garry's Goofs

by Garry Bushell

To Benny Hill, Sid James and Barbara Windsor.

Thanks to Kelvin MacKenzie.
And to Carol, Julie, Danny, and Robert.
But above all, thank you to the loyal readers of The Sun
for spotting the majority of these collected clangers.
What a dirty-minded lot you are!
PS ``Bon chance''
to Comrade
Jo Jo.

"It's easy enough to be happy when life rolls along like a song, but a man's worthwhile if he can smile when everything's going wrong."

Saddam Hussein, 1991.

INTRODUCTION

To ERR is human, but to really muck things up you need a TV personality.

There isn't a celebrity in the world who hasn't opened their mouth and put their foot right in it at least once in their career.

And there are those, like sports commentators, who by the nature of their job, tend to talk first and think about what they have said later.

Since I started collecting my Garry's Goofs back in 1987, I have found that breakfast telly presenters are the most frequent 'offenders'.

When Kathy Tayler was the star of TVam, her name was rarely out of my column. Not because of her interviewing skills or her lovely looks, but because she suffered from 'autocue interruptus'. She had so much trouble sticking to her script that I was tempted to rename my goofs 'Kath's Gaffes' in her honour.

Who could forget the time when she welcomed Frank Sinatra as "Hank"? Or repeatedly called Trudie Styler "Judy"?

Kathy was also prone to coming out with strange statements like: **"This is the time of year when all men get hot under the trousers."** In one month alone, she managed to introduce actor William Shatner as **"Captain Kirk of Star Check fame"** and call Karl Howman from Brush Strokes "the star of Bread Strokes."

Lord knows what would have happened if she'd ever had to talk about Friar Tuck!

More recently, Kath's place as TVam's Golden Goofer has been taken by luscious weathergirl Ulrika Jonsson - despite stiff competition from Mike **"How fatal is it?"** Morris.

In one memorable week, Ulrika stunned viewers by revealing **"We've just got time for a quick one"** and **"We had it yesterday after the news."** She was talking about her weather forecast, naturally. And it was the rain Ulrika was on about when she announced: **"We just can't get enough of it."** More recently Ulrika was discussing Harry Enfield's comedy when she told him: **"I was enjoying it as much as I did last night." "Oh dear,"** said her TVam colleague Richard 'Wolfman' Keys, **"I hope Garry Bushell isn't watching."** Hard luck, chaps - I was!

Once you get in the habit of looking for goofs, you'll find them everywhere. I was in Southend when I noticed a sign on the side of a portaloo which seemed to be inviting passers-by to **"stop and drain cock"**.

While an advert in the Pets Corner of the Bury Journal boasted: **'Village Studios - have your pets shot professionally.'**

A jewellery shop in Lewisham, South London used to have this sign in its window:
'Why go elsewhere to be cheated when you can come here?'

And I once saw a notice on a huge electrical generator which gravely warned passers-by: **'DANGER! To touch these wires will result in instant death - anyone found doing it will be severely prosecuted.'**

Telegrams are another clanger-spotter's paradise. Bob Monkhouse once told me the true story of a pregnant woman who ran into the Aberdeen telegraph office and told the operator that her husband had gone off to London to have a banner made for the Church Christmas Bazaar and Pageant. But she had forgotten to tell him how large the banner should be, or which hymnal words should be used on the inscription. She finally sent him the following telegram:

'ANDREW McALLAN, ST PANCRAS HOTEL, LONDON; DEAR ANDREW, UNTO US A SON IS BORN, TWO FEET WIDE AND EIGHT FEET LONG.'

Even national newspapers aren't immune from the disease. Who could forget headline cock-ups like **'Man Found Dead In Graveyard'**?

But written howlers are no substitute for classic verbal clangers.

David Coleman is the most famous example of foot-in-mouth disease. His frequent bloopers were dubbed 'Colemanballs' by Private Eye, the former satirical magazine, after he came out with comments like this one from a race at the 1976

Olympics: **"The big Cuban opened his legs and showed his class."**

Anyone can make a Colemanball, and the Eye have issued a whole series of collections, much to David's delight.

So what is the difference between a Colemanball and a classic Garry's Goof?

Simple. It's all in the mind . . . or more exactly in the filthy minds of the great British public.

Whereas Colemanballs tend to feature commentators, telly experts and news-men talking gibberish, Garry's Goofs are essentially rooted in the traditional English love of double meanings. They are a celebration of the innuendo, the unintentional double entendre - many revolving around the multitude of interpretations that can be made of the innocent little word 'it'. As in "If I let something slip out, will you hold it against me?"

Garry's Goofs will be enjoyed by everyone who ever giggled when a male star told an interviewer that he was **"getting very big Down Under"**.

My all-time favourite was this gem from cricket commentator Brian Johnstone. He was talking about Michael Holding and Peter Willey during a Test match when he goofed: "The bowler's Holding, the batsman's Willey."

I make no apology for the fact that most of

my goofs are vulgar, saucy, and unlikely to appeal to ladies called Whitehouse. Like most people raised on Carry On films and Benny Hill, I relish this sort of traditional English sauce.

Its roots go right back to Chaucer, and flourished in our grandparents' days via salty seaside postcards, most brilliantly in the work of Donald McGill.

This was a rib-tickling world peopled by comic caricatures: nervous newly-weds, drunks with crimson hooters, wimpish husbands, ginormous wives with breasts like zeppelins, and dolly birds with more curves than Brands Hatch. A world where a small boy, hidden from his father's view by the man's own beer belly, would naturally prompt his dad to announce: "I've lost my little Willie." Where you could bet that if a woman shop assistant with an ample cleavage were hanging up pheasants, a bloke would tell his mate: **"You can't beat a bird with a nice meaty chest."** And where a man with his trousers round his ankles in an optician's would of course be told by his lady examiner: **"No no Mr Smith. I said, could I see your worn *spectacles*!"**

It found an echo in the British Music Hall, in the comedy of immortal stars like Marie Lloyd and Max Miller, who abandoned his plans to marry a fan-dancer after she damaged her fan . . . It was Max, the cheeky chappie, who told the story of how he was making his way up a narrow hill road until he found a pretty girl blocking his route. What happened? Obvious, isn't it? He tossed himself off . . .

Kept alive in the superb Carry On film series, the humble double meaning lives on and thrives today in areas as diverse as Viz comics and Barry Humphries' crude creation Sir Les Patterson, who always insists on a warm hand upon his entrance.

This modest collection stands proudly in that vulgar but vital tradition. And I believe that the best of these howlers deserve to be remembered for just as long as the classic seaside postcards.

Garry's Goofs are a constant reminder that we all make mistakes. Even me. Why only last week I was on a radio show and I stated, quite reasonably I thought, that I wasn't interested in getting involved in politics with a big P.

Now why, I wonder, did that make the studio engineer start giggling?

GARRY BUSHELL, 13th March 1992

Garry's Goofs

Golf commentator Richie Benaud came up with a classic howler during the 1989 British Masters tournament when he revealed: **"Notices are appearing at courses telling golfers not to lick their balls on the greens."**

Chain Letters presenter Allan Stewart was discussing a 6ft 5in contestant called Richard when he told two women competitors: **"That's enough Dick for both of you."**

Desmond Morris opened the door of the gents toilet at a zoo on Animal Roadshow to show Sarah Kennedy the beautiful birds inside. **"There's been a cockatoo in there,"** he told her.

Racing commentator Julian Wilson was discussing Goodwood jockeys when he told trainer Josh Gifford: **"I suppose the best ride around the place is your daughter."**

After comparing real life copper Ron Caddon to the fictional cops in The Bill, TVam's Mike Morris goofed: **"We need more Rons to join our police force."**

During a snooker match, commentator Jack Karnehm remarked: **"This is a very difficult shot as there's just 1½ inches between the balls."**

Judy Spiers was interviewing a wine expert on Pebble Mill about his experiences on a nudist beach when she said: **"Now tell the audience what popped up."**

Blockbusters host Bob Holness was asking about a contestant's mascot, a gift from a pal, when he goofed: **"Does your friend always give you one before you appear on TV?"**

They were talking about infertility on The Time. . . The Place when a lady in the audience protested: **"I'm fed up - everyone is having a poke at us."**

David Coleman was talking about Linford Christie's finishing power during the Tokyo World Championships when he observed: **"He's got a habit of pulling it out when it matters."**

Steve Ryder was covering the U.S. Masters golf when he remarked: **"Ballesteros felt much better today after a sixty-nine."** I'm not at all surprised.

Classic gaffe from Tommy Puett: **"The 16th-century four-poster bed was originally owned by Mick Jagger and Marianne Faithfull."**

Edward Kennedy was talking about his rape-charge nephew William Kennedy Smith when he said: **"I don't believe it - all the family love Willie."**

Harry Carpenter on heavyweight boxer Gary Mason: **"Oh what a good left hook - and Mason can throw them with either hand."**

Snooker commentator Clive Everton was talking about Steve James's use of a cue rest when he goofed: **"His tackle is coming out to its full length."**

Peter Alliss on Rivero's golf drive: **"Gosh, what an enormous one for such a little chap."**

Cricketer Richie Richardson shot up in pain after being struck in the wedding tackle during a vital Test match. Richie Benaud was commentating on the over when he goofed: **"That's two balls gone - Lewis to continue bowling."**

Michael Aspel put his foot in it during Billy Wright's This Is Your Life when he said: **"Sadly Lev Yashin had his leg amputated recently. But it didn't stop him from hopping on a plane to be here tonight."**

A Bolex is a make of camera, which is why golf commentator Peter Alliss told the photographer who was blocking his view:
"Move your Bolex to one side, there's a good chap."

Chris Tarrant was trying to help a female contestant name a famous motor-racing commentator. The answer was Murray Walker so Chris said:
"I'll give you a clue, his name sounds like something hard that tastes good when you suck it." "Ah," she replied.
"It must be Dickie Davies."

Mariella Frostrup was discussing a helicopter pilot on Video View when she informed viewers:
"He's ever so good at handling his chopper."

Big Jack Charlton was talking about taking a shot at goal when he said:
"Giannini should have shot himself."

The new stand at Doncaster race course took Brough Scott's breath away. **"My word,"** he said, **"Look at that magnificent erection."**

A guest was discussing hair styles on This Morning when he goofed: **"All brides like a bit of body before they get married."**

Richard Whiteley was talking about the length of a word on Countdown when he said: **"I'll get my little thing out and measure it."**

Weatherman Bill Giles was discussing stormy weather in the east of Britain when he revealed: **"The strongest winds will be around the backside."**

David Coleman was talking about rugby action, not the streaker shown on Question Of Sport, when he observed: **"Look at that lovely tackle."**

B ob Monkhouse was talking about the top prize on The $64,000 Question when he cuddled a female contestant and told her: **"You are now one step away from the big one."**

Kingsley Amis was discussing critics on Antenna when he said: **"I like a little poke now and then."**

Racing commentator John Francome was talking about an oddly-named French race when he goofed: **"If you can get that out at nine in the morning you can get anything out."**

Here's an extraordinary statement from Go Fishing's John Wilson, who said: **"While I've got my rod out, let's have a look at the size of my waggler. I've got a 12-inch waggler."** He meant his float, of course.

CLASSIC
COLEMAN CLANGERS

A Tribute To The Original
Guvnor of the Goof

"For those watching who haven't got
television sets, the live commentary is
on Radio Two."

"That's the fastest time ever run - but it's
not as fast as the world record."

"This man could be a black horse."

" The late start is due to the time."

"And there go the two leaders -
Boutayeb, Aouita and Baccouche."

"She's not Ben Johnson,
but then who is?"

"He is even smaller in real life than
he is on the track."

"We estimate, and this isn't an
estimation, that Greta Waltz is eighty
seconds behind."

"This race is all about racing."

"The news from the javelin is that it
was won by that winning throw
we saw earlier."

Much-married Des O'Connor amazed viewers by announcing: **"I can screw myself into the ground on a good night."**
Of course, he was referring to his impressive prowess on the dance floor.

Cricket commentator Tom Graveney on Curtly Ambrose's bowling: **"The old fella can still get it up when he wants to."**

Virginia Wade was talking about Wimbledon services when she remarked: **"As a lady doubles player, you must expect to handle a few hard balls."**

Kay Burley, on Sky News, talking about the jogging superstar: **"Fans tried to get close to Madonna, only to be fended off by her bouncers."** Let's chest hope she meant her bodyguards.

The Sun's own slimming queen Sally Ann Voak was talking about John Suchet's belly on News At One when she said: **"I'm sure you have a little bulge down there, John."**

Mike Rutherford was reviewing Phil Collins's dancing technique when he noted: **"He does it very fast for 35 seconds and then it's all over."**

Stunning weathergirl Ulrika Jonsson was actually discussing the new 5p coin when she came out with this mind-boggling statement: **"I was playing with it for ages, but I found it was too small. It kept slipping through my fingers. I prefer a big one."**

Racing commentator John McCririck slipped up when he told viewers: **"There's been some talk that Arousel is in season - and bookmakers are keen on laying her."**

After beating Willie Carson in the Ascot Gold Cup, Walter Swinburn remarked: **"I went out and got the measure of Willie."**

Talking about a motorbike rider and his 750cc bike at the Shell Supercup, Barry Nutley said: **"Presumably he'll never get his leg over anything bigger."**

Celebrity contestant Tim Rice came up with the word 'panties' on Countdown. Richard Whiteley turned to Carol Vorderman and sternly told her: **"Let's have panties down, Carol."**

Cricket commentator Tony Lewis was discussing the day-light when he observed: **"I believe it's got a little darker since the Indians came out."**

Murphy's Cup commentator John Helm was remarking on golfers' nerves when he said: **"Eamonn Darcy had one of the biggest knee-tremblers of all time."**

Weathergirl Ulrika Jonsson hit a funny note when she told a musician guest on TVam:
"I hear you've got a very unusual instrument on your lap."

Judy Finnigan was talking about massaging conditioner into the hair when she goofed:
"Right, so a good rub every day is what we all need."

On BBC1's Churchill series, Winston's former secretary was reflecting on how the great man constructed his speeches when she said:
"He tried and tried all night long, but he just could not make it come."
Wonder if Paddy Ashdown has the same problem. . .

An unfortunate slip of the tongue led Going For Gold's Henry Kelly to promise one female contestant:
"forty seconds on the cock."

Judi Spiers was talking about snacks on the Valentine's Day edition of Pebble Mill when she said:
"Lovers want something quick they can grab with one hand."

Who would have guessed Beatrice Hillyer was discussing the availability of fresh water in Baghdad when she informed TVam viewers: **"Just after the liberation, I was getting it twice a day in my hotel room."**

Boxer Lennox Lewis on his beaten opponent Mike Weaver: **"I took my time until he exposed himself, and then I let him have it."**

TVam presenter Lorraine Kelly managed to out-goof her clanger-prone colleagues by revealing: **"If I ever get pregnant, I shall be lying on the settee with my feet up."**

Michael Parkinson was talking about a film title on Give Us A Clue when he told Lisa Goddard: **"If you think that was a long one, I've got a bigger one for you."**

Jack Nicklaus, explaining why a golfer was standing back from the tee in the U. S. Open, said: **"The flies are bothering him - they land on the balls and up his shaft."**

Anne Gregg was talking about a rhinoceros on Holiday 91 when she remarked: **"Ooh, hasn't he got a beautiful horn on him?"**

Golf commentator Alec Hay on Nick Faldo: **"His feet will be in the rough, but his balls are on the fairway."**

Trevor Brooking on the soccer style of Anders Limpar: **"He likes to get an early feel."**

CLASSIC CLANGER
Trevor Francis: **"I think the Italians have got their hands cut out tonight."**

Bruno Brookes was comparing his height with a contestant's on Love At First Sight, when he goofed: **"I'm proud of my extra half inch."**

A Daytime Live interviewer was talking about A Midsummers Night Dream when she told Roy Hudd: **"I'll see your Bottom in Regents Park this summer."**

Sun girl Sally Brockway got all flustered when she was telling Bruno Brookes about her hobby, Lambada dancing, on Love At First Sight. She goofed: **"I normally have ten partners every night."**

Telly chef Anton Mosimann must have made many an eye water when he said: **"For my strudel pastry I have to thank my very hot balls."** Thankfully he was talking about his stainless steel BOWLS.

Nick Skelton was talking about getting a tea bag in a cup on You Bet when he confessed: **"In the mornings, I can't get it in from six inches."**

Jilly Cooper was talking about gardening on Stars And Their Gardens when she observed: **"Men like to stick things up, and women like them lying down."**

Carol Baxter was trying to
identify an apple when she opined:
"And this one tastes like Cox."

Asked how Robert Maxwell was feeling in the days before his death, Daily Mirror editor Richard Stott told ITN: **"He was in a very buoyant mood."**

Here's a mind-boggling quote from a London local news reader:

"Twenty per cent of women like men with short legs, 30 per cent like men with long legs, and the other 50 per cent prefer something in between."

Timmy Mallett was explaining how
Aborigines painted on TVam when he said:
**"The men would sit here,
and this is where the women
ground their nuts."**

Here's a right royal ricket from
HRH Prince Philip:
**"The grouse are in absolutely
no danger from people
who shoot grouse."**

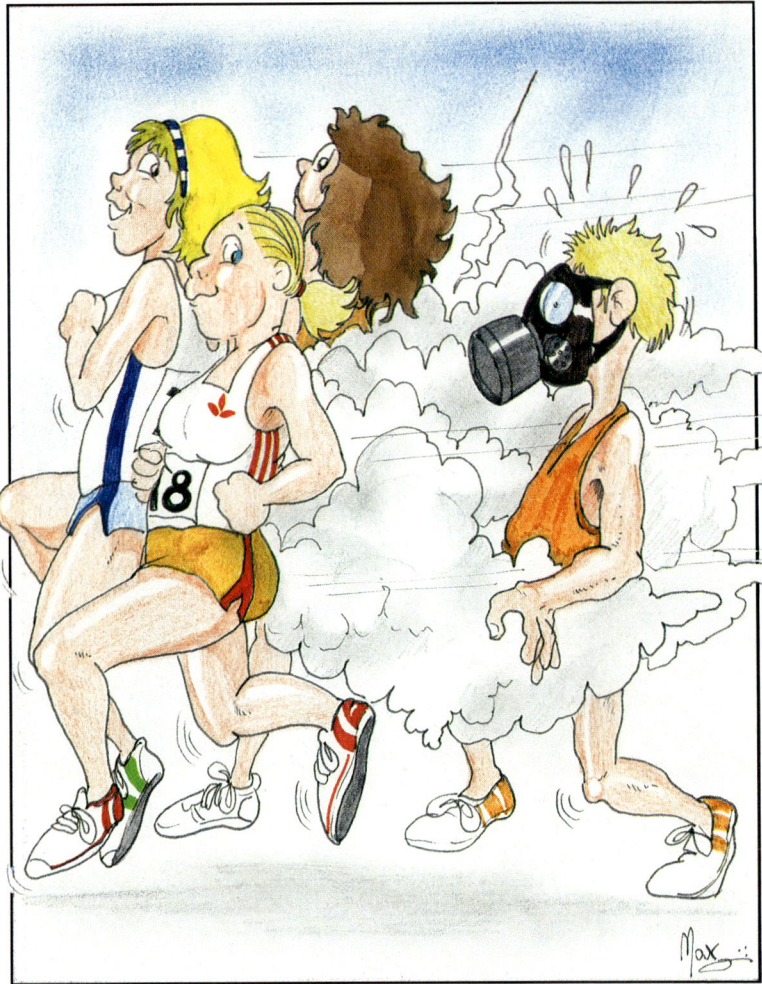

TV commentator during
the mixed marathon:
**"Many of the female contestants are
getting nearer the front and
starting to break wind."**

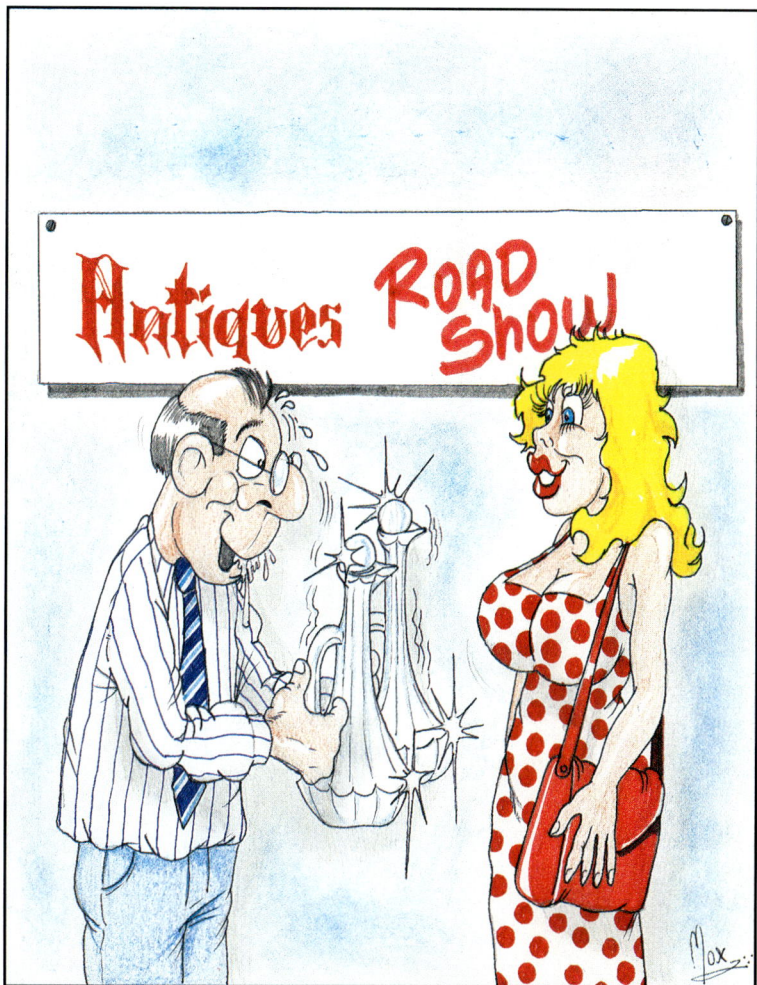

An Antiques Roadshow expert was
talking about two glass decanters, not
their attractive owner, when he goofed:
**"That's the nicest pair
I've seen in ages."**

BBC newscaster Debbie Hall tickled
Breakfast Time viewers when she said:
**"Horse trainer Fred Winter
is in hospital in
a stable condition."**

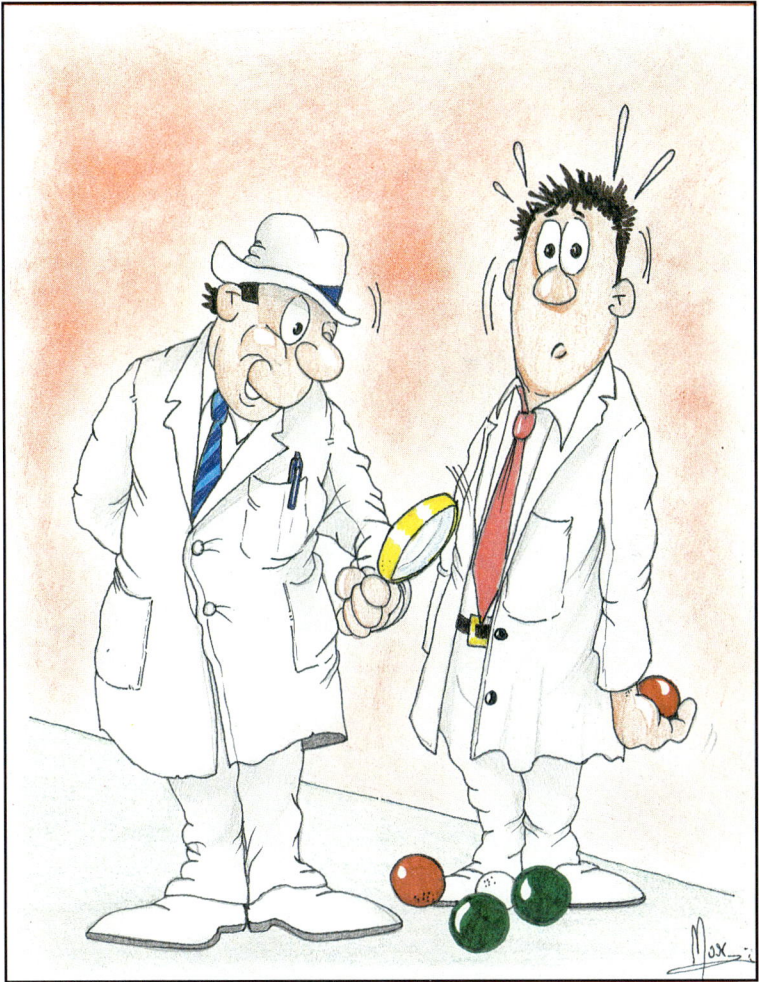

During a dispute about distances in the
1987 CIS Bowls championship, the ref
hollered at a startled assistant:
"One inch, Willie."
Poor old Willie.

Nice goof during This Week's examination of private health care when the reporter explained that the patient:

"Would receive a detailed computerised bill for everything from his replacement plastic knee joint down to his cotton wool balls."

Antique expert speaking on
Sky's Satellite Shop:
**"I know Catherine Howard was one of
Henry VIII's wives, but I don't know
if she survived his chopper."**

During the 1990 World Cup, Barry Davies
said of one of the Holland team:
**"I wonder how he feels,
his first game in a Dutch cap."**

A vet on Daytime Live goofed when
he told Floella Benjamin:
**"If tortoises don't eat enough in the
summer, when they hibernate
they wake up dead."**

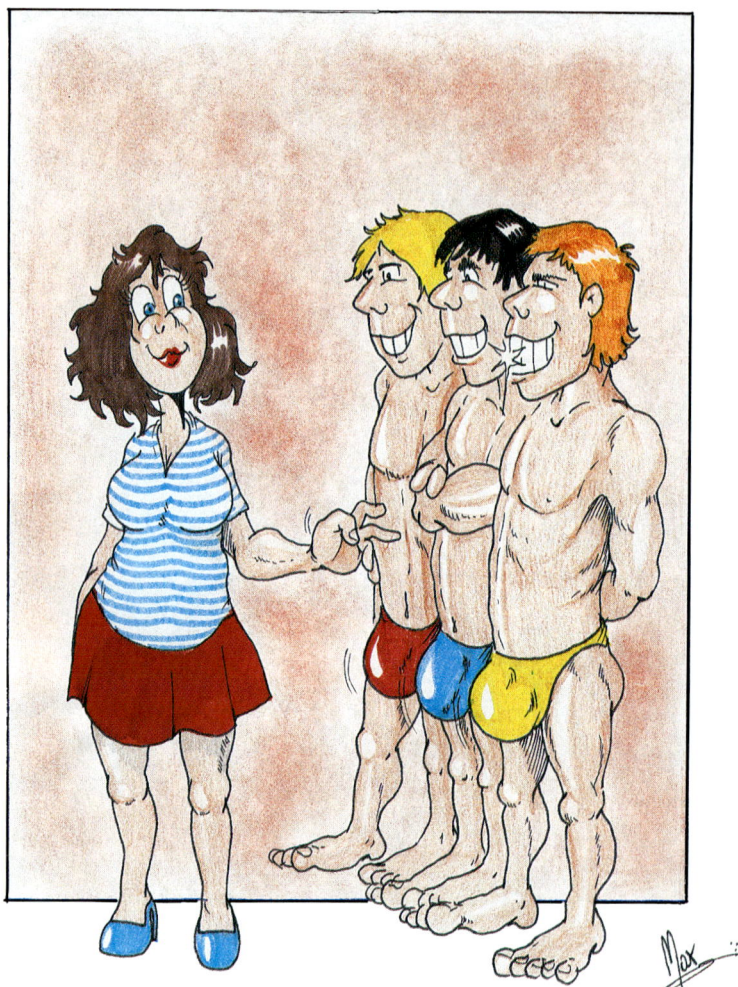

Mike Smith asked a mum
on No Kidding:
**"I hear you've been to see
the Chippendales - did anything
about them stick out in particular?"**

Weathergirl Ulrika Jonsson was talking
about overnight snowfalls when she said:
**"I had a good eight inches
last night."**

Rob Curling goofed on the
BBC news when he said:
**"A police officer from Kent will
appear in court tomorrow on a charge
of supplying cannabis after
a joint investigation."**

Roy Walker to an understandably nervous contestant on Catchphrase: **"We're putting the money up, you're behind."**

Richard Madeley to Julian Lennon on This Morning: **"Do you think you owe your success to what's in your genes?"**

Classic own goal from Graeme Souness: **"You cannot guarantee a thing in this game. All you can guarantee is disappointment."**

Asked how old she would be this birthday on This Morning, pop warbler Dannii Minogue replied: **"Twenty-double figures . . ."** What a loss she is to MENSA!

Anne Diamond introducing Hilary Jones on TV Weekly: **"Here is the doctor half the women in Britain would love to be under."**

Nick Gillingham might have taken more care of his words when he described a male swimmer on Question Of Sport as:
"The greatest-ever breast stroker."

Ted Lowe was talking about snooker ref Ted Williams's measuring equipment when he said:
"And now he's got his little thing on the table to measure it."

Racing commentator Derek Thompson was discussing a trainer's bets when he goofed:
"Mrs Knight certainly likes a little touch now and again."

Carol Vorderman was talking about a number puzzle on Countdown when she told a stunned male contestant:
"I can't wait to see the size of your big one."

> ## CLASSIC CLANGER
> Man City skipper Paul Power:
> **"I can't promise anything,
> but I can promise 100 per cent."**

Kathryn Holloway was showing off her engagement ring on TVam when she goofed: **"It was so romantic. He just took it out and put it on the table in Soho."**

Ross King, discussing relays with champion runner Phil Redmond: **"Well Phil, tell us about your amazing third leg."**

Richard Whiteley startled the female champion on Countdown by telling her: **"Your new challenger has come all the way from Plymouth to try and knock you off."** Game chap!

Garden Club presenter Rebecca Pow was talking about onions when she told Roy Lancaster: **"I see you're holding an extra large one in your hand there, Roy."**

Noel Edmonds was referring to an NTV stunt on Noel's House Party when he remarked: **"This time last week I had a woman on the carpet."**

Darts ace Jocky Wilson scored 180, prompting commentator Sid Waddell to exclaim: **"Oh, what a time to pull it out!"**

Gay Byrne to actor Kenneth Branagh: **"I want to know what it feels like to play with your wife."**

TVam viewers were taken aback when weathergirl Ulrika Jonsson confided: **"I'm having problems with boyfriend withdrawal."**

CLASSIC CLANGER

**"I've got ten pairs of training
shoes - one for every day
of the week."** - Sam Fox.

Julio Iglesias on Willie Nelson:
"Always I am so grateful for Willie."

Michael Barrymore was asking a
contestant about the time she lost her
husband when he said: **"So you went
looking for Dick at the bus station?"**

Classic cock-up from Guy
Michelmore: **"Many supporters
say they wouldn't stand for
all-seater stadiums."**

Snooker ace Steve Davis thrashed
Nigel Bond and then goofed:
**"It was actually a game played in
three halves."**

Jimmy Greaves talking about the Northampton v. Southampton match on Saint And Greavsie: **"It will be the biggest hampton that wins."**

Dr Keith Mumby was discussing allergies on Granada's Up Front when he said: **"I've come up here tonight to publicly expose myself."**

Poor old Arthur Billitt sounded like Julian Clary on Gardening Time when he revealed: **"Whenever I see a pansy I get really excited."**

Brendan Foster, commentating on a lady runner in the Great North Run on Grandstand, goofed: **"She looks like she's had a hard one today."**

Phillip Schofield was trying to help kids writing in French on Going Live when he said: **"You must try harder with your French letters."**

CLASSIC HOWLERS
THE BEST OF DAN MASKELL

Legendary commentator Dan Maskell was the voice of tennis for 43 years. But much-loved Dan was as famous for serving up gaffes as for his wealth of tennis memories. Here are my ten favourite Maskell Mis-serves:

"And here come the Gullikson twins, both from Wisconsin."

"Roscoe Tanner is one of the great runners-up of all time. No man could have played better."

"He slips, but manages to regroup himself."

On a doubles partnership: "The British boys are adopting the attacking position - Cox up."

"There is Peter Graf, Steffi's father, with his head on his chin."

"When Martina is tense, it helps her to relax."

"Oh my word, a glorious shot! Would have been a winner if it had gone over the net."

"Nobody has worked harder than Gottfried to get to the top, and certainly nobody more so than Borg."

"Oh! That cross court angle was so acute it didn't exist."

"Borg v McEnroe. A feast of tennis in store. I can predict either of them winning."

Jim Rosenthal was talking about soccer balls on Saint And Greavsie when he slipped up and said: **"You can't afford to drop 'em in front of Maradona."**

Something must have impressed Blind Date winner Hannah about her trip to Denmark for she suddenly exclaimed: **"That is huge! I've never seen one as big as that before."** Don't worry Cilla. She was talking about a giant caterpillar. . .

An American balloonist was telling Fred Talbot about his prize-winning vessel on Granada Tonight when he admitted: **"I find it very difficult to get it up early in the mornings."**

David Coleman on Linford Christie's sprinting prowess: **"Just when it mattered, Christie found an extra two inches which proved vital."**

Big boob from Jenny Murray on Daytime Live: **"If you need something to take your mind off breast-feeding, the place to be is Bristol."**

A hold-up to a pre-match shoot-in during the 1986 World Cup prompted Trevor Brooking to comment: **"I bet the Italians are itching to get their balls out."**

Bread's Jonathan Morris was discussing his panto when he revealed: **"One flick of the fairy's wand and Dick starts to rise."**

Nina Myskow was telling Clive Anderson about discrimination when she remarked: **"We women have taken the sharp end for long enough."** And Nina more than most!

I don't normally include dialogue in my goofs, but I bet the Brookside writers didn't mean it to sound so saucy when Max admired Ron's new fence and asked: **"What do you think of your husband's erection, Mrs Dixon?"**

A bird watcher slipped up on the Software Show when he told a lady computer expert: **"You've got Great Tits nearly all the time."**

Guy Michelmore was talking about river fishing when he observed: **"The mere mention of it is enough to make some men go weak and start fumbling for their tackle."**

SOCCER GOOFS

Britain's soccer commentators all played a blinder during the 1990 World Cup. But John Motson won my Golden Boot In The Mouth award for these two cracking clangers: **" He's making a meal of that injured arm."** And: **"They're taking him off because he's been carrying that leg for some time."**

Here's how the runners-up scored: Bobby Charlton: **"It could go either way, or it might even be a draw."**

John Helm: **"The Costa Ricans are holding themselves up."**

Barry Davies: **"He gets a standing ovation for that. . . even from those who are seated."**

Elton Welsby: **"The West German team has the most players we have ever seen."**

Ron Atkinson: **"He didn't miss it, he just didn't make contact."**

Alan Parry: **"He'll have to be very careful because he's sitting on a yellow card."**

Judi Spiers was talking about male hunks at a Mr Telethon muscleman contest when she said: **"Well, we've seen the little tinkers in their trunks."**

Walter Swinburn goofed when he told Channel 4 Racing: **"Punters don't realise the amount of wind we get up our backsides during the final furlong of the race."** No wonder my jockeys always ride a stinker!

A man and woman duo's score on Opportunity Knocks prompted this quote from Les Dawson: **"Sixty-nine, a great speciality act."**

Golf commentator Peter Alliss was discussing Nick Faldo's shapely female caddie when he remarked: **"If Nick wins, I wonder if he'll give her something big."**

Dr John MacCormack on TVam:
**"Women are more prone to
pre-menstrual tension."**

Marti Caine went on Family
Fortunes as Dick Whittington.
Les Dennis told her:
"You've got a prize Dick."

Zandra Rhodes was talking about
Willie Rushton's house on Through
The Keyhole when she goofed:
**"Now I can go round the panel's
homes and inspect Willie's."**

Countdown's curvy Carol Vorderman was talking about numbers again when she said: **"I've got a couple of nice big ones on the side."**

'This Morning' cook Susan Brookes was showing off her Easter cake when she said: **"The only problem is when you cut it your balls drop off."**

Barry Manilow, describing his effect on women: **"When you wriggle your bottom it's like the second coming."**

Snooker commentator John Pulman was remarking on a shot from Robert Markham when he said: **"Another six inches and he'd have been perfect."**

With snooker ace Steve Davis three frames down, commentator John Pulman goofed: **"Davis needs the pot badly, he's very unsettled."**

Lucinda Green, discussing a mare on Grandstand, observed: "**She's very game, a lovely ride, but it looks like she hasn't seen a big one for a couple of years.**"

Asked on Kilroy if she had used a condom during sex, an unmarried mum retorted: "**Yes, but there must have been a prick in it.**"

Strange quote from Harry Carpenter during the 1990 Commonwealth boxing finals: "**It must be tiring to have a man constantly on top of you.**"

A mum was talking about impressions when she explained to Oprah Winfrey why she had chosen a young hunk as a suitable date for her daughter. **"I liked the feel he gave me,"** she said.

Here's a holy howler from Deacon Sue Izzard. Talking about female priests on Reportage, Sue opined: **"Maybe it's going to come through people exposing themselves to women in front of churches."**

Joan Bakewell, discussing artificial insemination with an ex-con on Heart Of The Matter, asked: **"Did the other inmates make it hard for you?"**

Nicky Fox was telling TVam's Mike Morris about the heat in Kenya, and not the perils of nude sunbathing, when she remarked: **"It's no fun having sun-stroke in the bush."**

Asked how long he would continue
riding a motorbike on Mavis Catches
Up, Malcolm Forbes replied:
**"As long as I can get my
leg over, why stop?"**

Mastermind host Magnus
Magnusson was left feline daft
when he goofed: **"The Turkish Van,
Abyssinian and British Blue are
all types of what ca. . . . animal?"**

Schoolboy quoted on a
Thames News report on education:
**"The Bengal Lancers were
an army of white officers
with black privates."**

Presenter Peter Machan was discussing scraping the hulls of boats on Tomorrow's World when he said: **"There's nothing like it - wind in your face and a clean bottom."**

Is Ben Elton as "politically correct" as he would like us to think?
Here are some of his views on safe sex, as told to Terry Wogan:
"Even if the condom in your purse was approaching the sell-by date, it would still be worth having it."

Great goof from a phone-in caller called Linda during a This Morning discussion of women's fertility.
She said: **"I was under the doctor and wallop, I became pregnant."**

Strange confession from Swansea MP Alan Williams: **"We'd like to get Mrs Thatcher on the floor of the Commons for half an hour to see what her reaction would be."**

Julian Wilson said of an Ascot runner on Grandstand: **"If you look closely you can see he has all the attributes of a great stallion."**

Touring can be exhausting, according to Julian Lloyd Webber. He told This Morning viewers: **"If you take your wife with you, you're on top of each other all the time."**

Ian St John on Liam Brady: **"What a lovely left foot... he's always had it."**

John Sessions was discussing his abilities as a mimic when he remarked: **"I really don't have what it takes to do Liz Taylor."**

Reg Gutteridge on boxer Mike Weaver: **"He might be a bit slow on his legs, but he can still bang a bit."**

Howzat for a howler! Jack Bannister bowled a googly when he remarked: **"The Australians really fancy Graham Gooch around the short-leg area."**

Tom O'Connor to Dinah Sheridan on Crosswits: **"It seems like only yesterday that we were on the game together."**

Timmy Mallet should really get a grip on himself. When star guest Kylie Minogue got a wrong answer in his mallet quiz on Wacaday, tiresome Timmy told her: **"I think you deserve a bonk for that."**

TVam's Richard Keys was talking about retrieving lost hamsters when a caller came on with this useful advice: **"Just shake your nuts under the floorboards and they'll come running."**

CLASSIC CLANGER

Ron Atkinson: **"I'm going to make a prediction - it could go either way."**

Jim Rosenthal was talking about Peter Beardsley's soccer technique when he goofed: **"Beardsley is now on top and working hard to get it in."**

Strange question from Des Lynam to Christine Truman: **"How do you feel about the men's tackle this year?"** Thankfully he was talking about male tennis fashions.

TV chef Glyn Christian said of a large Royal show bull and its equally huge lady owner: **"Just look at the size of this beast. I don't think I've ever seen one as big. Oh! I mean the bull!"**

Top Of The Pops presenter Anthea Turner on Cher's stay at Number One: **"Nobody's been able to knock her off."**

US wrestling commentator Gorilla Monsoon was talking about the engagement ring WWF star Macho Man had bought the lovely Miss Elizabeth when he goofed: **"He's building up his confidence, he's reaching for it, he's getting it out..."**

Handyman Doug Smillie was putting up shelves on Bazaar when he startled Nerys Hughes by smiling at her and saying: **"We're ready for screwing now."**

Bazaar chef Lesley Waters was talking about baking beef cobblers when she explained: **"First you must get your cobblers and brush them with milk."**

Miriam Stoppard was hosting a discussion on the new x-rated satellite Adult Channel on People Today. Just as a clip of a couple getting passionate was flashed up on the screen, Miriam rather alarmingly asked: **"How big do you think it will get?"**

Ron Pickering on a London Marathon runner: **"He's letting his legs do the running."**

TVam's Mike Morris was discussing White House interest in astrology when he said: **"Ronald Reagan? Oh yes, he's an aquarium."**

Brian Moore was talking about Pierre Littbarski's throw-in during the West Germany v Italy football match when he remarked: **"For a little man it's really quite a long one.'**

Goof, set and match to tennis commentator Dan Maskell for serving up this howler: **"Lendl returned that well, but created an enormous hole for himself down his backside."**

US newsreader Dan Adams got his tongue in a twist at an awards ceremony when he said: **"Ladies and gentlemen, it is a great privilege to present to you now, the virgin of Governor's Island."**

Julian Jutt, commentating on the Ladies Giant Slalom from Albertville, said of gold medallist Wiberg: **"She is normally very powerful at the bottom."**

I had better explain that a Mrs Cox is a type of geranium, otherwise there is no telling what you would make of this superb goof from gardener Howard Drury on Midlands Gardening: **"Mrs Cox, a very good one indoors or out, good in a bed, good in a conservatory. I think Mrs Cox is one to have a go with."**

A farmer was telling London Weekend TV news about his sick cattle when he said: **"This poor cow will have to be put down within the week."** Unfortunately, the LWT boys were flashing up a picture of newscaster Pam Royal at the time!

On Through The Keyhole, the noble Lord Montagu told David Frost that part of his stately home was open to the public. David replied: **"Well, it was nice to see your private parts anyway."**

Here's a regal ricket from Tom Fleming, commentating on the Queen's 1988 birthday parade: **"You can see the Queen's carriage and the colonel's behind."**

When the West Indian cricket captain tried to attract a player's attention, commentator Richie Benaud excitedly remarked: **"And Viv Richards is giving Patrick Patterson the clap."**

Anneka Rice was talking about her helicopter pilot on the 1988 Telethon Treasure Hunt when she exclaimed: **"He's in an optimistic mood, he's got an extra-large chopper today."**

Asked about her nag's chances on Channel 4 Racing, jockey Jennie Goulding replied: **"I haven't ridden him, but George Duffield has been filling me in."**

Cilla Black was discussing
the height of a male dancer on
Surprise Surprise when she observed:
**"If you're going to have one,
have a big one."**

I hope Frank Bough was only
talking about his attempts to get off to
sleep in Holiday Outings when he said:
**"I've tried forty-seven positions in
five hours, but it's still no good."**

Brian Johnson was talking to
musician Harry Mortimer on Years
Ahead when he goofed: **"I know
you've brought your instrument with
you - I can see it between your legs."**

Douglas Hurd raised a few
eye-brows on Question Time
when he revealed: **"I spent most of
the day on a boat on the Thames
going up and down with the ladies."**

TV commentator at Goodwood:
**"There's a jockey down there
walking around on his feet."**

Tony Lewis, commentating
during the 1987 Pakistan-England
cricket Test, said: **"That's how
it looked in slow motion, but it
went a lot quicker than that."**

World Gymnastics Championship commentator: **"He is what Nadia Komanee and Olga Korbut were to mens' gymnastics."**

A bloke who had taken his teddy bear all around the world told viewers of The Time. . . The Place: **"This bear has circumcised the entire world."**

Commenting on a procession of different food on Daytime Live, Judi Spiers remarked: **"And now, bringing up the rear, we have prunes."**

Richard Whiteley stunned contestants on Countdown when he asked: **"Well, who wants to have a go with Carol?"**

Shock admission from Chicago Bears star Jim McMahon: **"Sometimes I feel so good my balls start to spiral."**

Chef Jill Myers goofed after making a chocolate pudding on Farmhouse Kitchen when she said: **"You can do it this way, but I've actually made this one sitting on the pan."**

Dietician Patrick Holford was talking about the oil content of food on Rosemary Conley's Diet And Fitness programme when he said: **"If you set fire to your nuts, you'll soon discover how much oil they contain."**

Blockbusters contestant to Bob Holness: **" I fancy a P now, please Bob."**

Commentator Robin Jackman on cricket ace Ian Botham: **"There's nothing Botham likes   better than a maiden or two under his belt."**

Judy Spiers told Dudley Moore on Pebble Mill: **"And this is where your career forked off. . ."** No wonder cuddly Dudley collapsed in hysterics!

Chiropodist Brian Berry was talking about ladies shoes on TVam when he said: **"The sooner women get them off the better."**

Ann Jones, commenting on the 1987 Ladies Doubles final at Wimbledon: **"How much better a doubles match is when all four players are alive."**

Two male contestants guessed a woman's age wrongly on Runway. Richard Madeley goofed: **"Elizabeth, they've both straddled you."**

Ted Lowe on Stephen Hendry's snooker prowess: **"There's Stephen showing us those long balls he's famous for."**

The night after the great winds in October 1987, lovely Lisa Maxwell turned to weathergirl Trish Williamson and asked: **"Well, what happened last night, was it a storm?"**

After an Open Air interview with Julian Pettifer about his new TV series about famous missionaries, Patti Coldwell told him: **"And good luck with your missionary position, Julian."**

Jean Rook meant to say "unselfconscious" when she told TVam's Anne Diamond: **"Mrs Gorbachev is always so totally unconscious."**

Over to the World Athletics Championship for this rather cruel remark from Dave Moorcroft: **"There are guys like Daley Thompson, Fatima Whitbread, and Steve Cram still to come."**

CLASSIC CLANGER

Brough Scott: **"When those stalls open the horses are literally going to explode."**

Dickie Davies, during the World Snooker Doubles: **"Graham particularly likes playing with tight balls. . . some of our players could do with a pair like that."**

"I am a housewife and mother," a contestant told Michael Barrymore on Strike It Lucky. **"Any children?"** asked Michael.

Daytime Live's Judi Spiers was interviewing a Taff teacher about the age when Welshmen take up rugby when she remarked: **"I've heard it said they're given balls when they're born."**

Was it only the rain BBC weatherman Michael Fish was discussing when he informed viewers: **"Some people might wake up tomorrow and find they've had an inch or two."** ?!?

Pattie Coldwell was talking on Open Air about a send-up of TV soaps when she goofed: **"Neighbours fans will be turning in their graves."**

Anneka Rice got all excited on Treasure Hunt when a Red Arrow pilot came in to land. **"Look look,"** she squawked, **"He's giving me a flash. . . Come on, give me another flash."** And he did too.

Snooker commentator John Pulman snookered himself when he remarked: **"These young lads carry their own extensions just like the pros. I wish I'd had one like that when I was their age."**

Des Lynam: **"The second
Nottingham Forest goal was
scored by Nigel Clough who
is the son of his dad."**

Classic quote from Miss World
organiser Julia Morley:
**"Miss World has always had
its fair share of knockers."**

Gardening expert Joe White
astonished Daytime Live viewers by
telling them: **"Remember this is the
time of year when you really must
get out in those gardens and it's
prick out every five to six inches."**

Jack Karnehm was commenting on Jimmy White's snooker technique when he observed: **"He really is the master of the slow screw."**

Darts commentator Tony Green demonstrated his exceptional grasp of metric measurements during the match between Bob Anderson and Bert Vlaardingerbroek, saying: **"Bob leans his 6ft 4in well forward and so does Bert who at 1.9 metres is well over three foot."**

On New Years Eve, 1987, BBC weatherman Bill Giles informed us: **"Tomorrow could be the mildest day of the year so far."**

Sam Fox boobed in a BBC interview when she said: **"I've always been a bit more maturer than what I am."**

When Mikhail Gorbachev met East German dictator Erich Honecker, ITN newsreader Sandy Gall informed us: **"He is the first Soviet bloc head to meet Mr Gorbachev."**

James Whale was hosting a discussion about depression when he asked a guest: **"And how did you feel when you committed suicide?"**

Classic quote from Ron Pickering who described US runner Harvey Glance as **"The black American sprinter with the white top and the black bottom."**

Ted Lowe on a Steve Davis snooker shot: **"Steve's long one doesn't come off."**

Sky At Night star Patrick Moore was discussing the size of telescope lenses when he informed viewers: **"Personally, I've got a very fine five inch."**

Judy Finnigan was talking about chocolate cakes on this year's Valentines Day edition of This Morning when she told cook Susan Brooks: **"I fancy more than just a little one, Susan."**

Gamesmaster presenter Dominik Diamond opened the show with this strange statement: **"You may be wondering what I am doing playing with my organ in church."**

Here's a Breakfast Time goof from one-time co-presenter Sally Magnusson: **"I spent three months on the red sofa with Frank, then I became pregnant."**

Shock confession from Alan Shearer about playing in the same England team as Gary Lineker: **"Yes, I like playing with Gary up front."**

Murray Walker, commentating on the South African Grand Prix: **"Senna's been staring at Patrese's rear end all afternoon."**

Cricket commentator Harry Blofeld: **"It's very difficult to read the scores between Abdul Qadir's balls."**

Pat Cash had thrashed his wife in a baseball computer game on Gamesmaster when Dominik Diamond commented: **"You started off well, then Pat started banging you all over the ground."** ...Later on the same show, he was discussing a new piece of software when he said: **"This new game will have all fans of flight simulators rubbing their helmets with glee."**

Dickie Davies miscued during a Cliff Thorburn and Dennis Taylor snooker match when he said: **"They're playing with each other for the first time, but they're happy."**

Chef Antony-Vorall Thomson was talking about preparing a dish on Hot Chef when he told his assistant Kate: **"No, no, I want you to come here and do what you did for me last night."**

Sarah Greene goofed on Going Live by asking Greg Benson from Home and Away: **"How long was there between Nobby's nuts and the boxer shorts?"** She was talking about his modelling career!

The narrator on BBC2 nature programme Sharks was talking about several male sharks trying to mate with one female when he said: **"It looks like they have some stiff competition."**

Dougie Donnelly, commentating
on World Bowls:
**"Clark will probably fire
at the head . . . yes, he's put some
strength into it . . .
OH! He's shot both his bowls off!"**

Classic clanger from Ray Illingworth
during the NatWest Trophy cricket
match. He commented:
**"Geoff Cook was hit in the
groin yesterday. . . it's obviously
stiffened up over night."**

Classic quote from Frank Bruno,
discussing the clash of heads
in the Honeyghan-Vaca fight:
**"That's cricket, 'Arry -
these things happen in boxing."**

Countdown's Richard Whitely
to two male contestants:
**"We are surrounded by ladies
today, so it's up to us men to
keep our end up."**

Action girl Anneka Rice
was talking about bunk
beds on Wish You Were Here?
when she wistfully remarked:
**"I wonder who's sleeping
on top of me tonight."**
There's a challenge for you!

Classic clanger from Jimmy Hill:
**"Italians spend a lot of money
to buy the best in their leagues,
for example Real Madrid."**

Elton Welsby on The Match:
**"If Leeds want to win,
I hope they know that they are going
to have to beat the goalkeeper."**

Quote from Thora Hird on Praise Be:
**"If Charles Wesley were alive today,
he would turn in his grave."**

Ulrika Jonsson:
**"This afternoon there will be
bright sunshine until after dark."**

With one player's bowl eight
inches from the jack during the
Waterloo Crown Green Bowls
Tournament, commentator
Harry Rigby remarked:
**"Look at that, he keeps
on licking his eight-inch balls."**

AND STILL THEY POUR IN . . .
HERE ARE SOME OF THE GOOFS THAT
I SPOTTED IN MARCH, 1992:

Desmond Lynam on Genoa's
first goal against Liverpool:
**"Some goals are so good,
they're... goals really."**

Ian St. John during the
Spurs v. Feyenord match:
**"Johnny Methold has been
wonderful. He's done everything
on the ground tonight."**

And finally how about this
clanger from David Coleman,
who was talking about the Swiss
two-man bob event at the Winter
Olympics when he said:
**"He's always fiddling with bobs in
the garage at the back of his house."**

CLASSIC CLANGER
Greg Norman:

"I owe a lot to my parents, especially my mother and father."

MORE Garry's Goofs are published every Wednesday in **'Bushell On The Box '**- Garry's TV column in

The Number One Sun.

You could win £20 by sending any howlers you hear on a postcard to:

**GARRY'S GOOFS,
THE SUN,
1, VIRGINIA STREET,
LONDON E1 9XP.**

MORE FROM GARRY BUSHELL

COMING this Autumn from Britain's top TV critic:

'THE BEST OF BUSHELL ON THE BOX'

It's the definitive A-Z of television, the toughest, funniest collection of telly reviews ever published.

What does Garry really think about TVam, Ben Elton, Julian Clary, James Whale, EastEnders and the bosses of the BBC and the ITV companies?

'THE BEST OF BUSHELL ON THE BOX' deflates the over-rated, punctures the pompous, and makes a proud stand for the best in popular television.

It's the book that shows why hard-hitting Garry Bushell is the most loved - and most hated - TV critic in Britain.

Will the stars dare to read it?
Can YOU bear to miss it?
Frank, fearless and funny,
'THE BEST OF BUSHELL ON THE BOX'
is published by
Kingsfleet this Autumn ...